Grandma Wants To Eat My Baby Sister!

To the shiniest apple of the bunch!
Jackie Jafarian Broad

Written by Jackie Jafarian Broad
Illustrated by Shielaugh Victoria Divelbiss

Copyright ©2008 by Jackie Jafarian Broad.
All rights reserved. No part of this book may be reproduced or transmitted
in any form by any means, electronic or mechanical, including photocopying, recording, or by any
information storage and retrieval system, without written permission in writing from the author.

Cassidy Cataloguing-in-Publication Data
Broad, Jackie Jafarian.
Grandma wants to eat my baby sister! / written by Jackie Jafarian Broad ;
illustrated by Shielaugh Victoria Divelbiss. -- Mill Valley, CA : Three Puppies Press, c 2008.
p. ; cm.
ISBN: 978-0-9820654-0-2
Audience: Ages 3-8.
Summary: Maddie misunderstands when Grandma says that her baby sister, Alyssa, is so delicious she wants
to "eat" her. At first, Maddie thinks she won't mind at all; but as she discovers Alyssa is actually fun to have
around, Maddie believes she has to stop Grandma-- before it is too late!

1. Figures of speech--Juvenile fiction. 2. Sibling rivalry--Juvenile fiction. 3. Grandmothers--Juvenile fiction.
4. Ballet dancing-- Juvenile fiction. 5. English language--Idioms--Juvenile fiction. 6. [Figures of speech--Fiction.
7. Jealousy--Fiction. 8. Grandmothers--Fiction. 9. Ballet dancing--Fiction.] I. Divelbiss, Shielaugh Victoria. II. Title.
PZ7 .B78084 2008
[Fic]--dc22 0811

The illustrations in this book were done in pitt artist pen and digitally colored.
The display lettering was set in Girls Are Weird.
The text type was set in Artcraft Regular.
Book design and jacket art by Shielaugh Victoria Divelbiss.

Book consulting and editing by Amy Novesky.
www.amynovesky.com

Manufactured in China by Global Interprint, Santa Rosa, California.

A funny thing happened on the way to growing up...™

Three Puppies Press™
Mill Valley, California
www.threepuppiespress.com

To my three "puppies" — Madelyn, Alyssa and Jared.
And to two very special grandmas — Nana (Soury Jafarian)
and Grandma B (Laura Broad).

Love you all to pieces! — JJB

To my lifelong best friend, Rachel, who is like my sister.
And to my mom and dad,
for always being so supportive (even
when I drew on the walls).

I'm just bananas for all of you! — SVD

Maddie had Grandma all to herself, and that was just the way she liked it. Maddie especially loved all the fun and wacky things Grandma would say.

When Maddie was scared to put her head under the water at swim lessons, Grandma said, "Don't be a chicken, Maddie, just do it!"

When Maddie said that writing her name was too hard, Grandma said, "Practice, and it'll be a piece of cake."

When Maddie couldn't believe it rained for a whole week straight, Grandma said, "This weather is just bananas!"

Everything was great.
Until she came along —
Maddie's baby sister,

Alyssa

Grandma was coming over to babysit, and Maddie couldn't wait! Finally, the doorbell rang and in breezed Grandma.

it's colder than frozen yogurt outside!"

"Okay, my little pumpkins, are we ready to have some fun tonight?" she asked.

"Grandma, want to see me dance? My recital is tomorrow!" said Maddie, twirling in her tutu.

"Wait a minute, cupcake. Will you look at her! Alyssa is crawling!" shouted Grandma.

"What a ham you are, Alyssa! And you smell so yummy!" Grandma laughed. "With those tender meaty legs, plump little fingers and rosy apple cheeks ... well I could just eat you up!

Good, I hope Grandma does eat you up, thought Maddie angrily. Sometimes, Maddie wished Alyssa would just disappear.

"I'm making my specialty for dinner tonight," Grandma said. "Spaghetti and meatballs!"

Suddenly, Maddie heard a roar!
It sounded like a bear, or a lion or ...

"My silly stomach," Grandma giggled. "I'm so hungry. I could eat a horse — or Alyssa!"

Maddie watched wide-eyed as Grandma lifted Alyssa's shirt and softly nibbled her belly!

"Alyssa is so delicious!"

At dinner, Grandma inhaled meatballs the size of golf balls, and sauce dribbled down her chin. Grandma really loves to eat — a lot! thought Maddie.

Alyssa was happy eating fistfuls of spaghetti. Then, she decided to throw a fistful at Grandma! Grandma gasped as the spaghetti hit her squarely in the face. Alyssa started to giggle uncontrollably. Then Maddie did too!

Alyssa's not so bad, Maddie thought.

Grandma shook her head and smiled.

"You girls are like two peas in a pod," she said, wiping her face.

Then Grandma reached for Alyssa with her long red claws.

Oh no! thought Maddie. Grandma had finished her spaghetti. Was Alyssa next?

"Look at those chubby rolls of sweetness," Grandma said, as she cleaned up Alyssa. "I know! Why don't we have some cutie pie for dessert? First, we'll put Alyssa in a pie shell, add some apple slices, some homemade whipped cream, and a cherry on top. What do you think, Maddie?"

I have to stop her!
Grandma wants to eat my baby sister!
That's what I think!

"Grandma, I don't feel so well. Let's skip dessert tonight," said Maddie.

"You never skip dessert," said Grandma, as she felt Maddie's forehead. "No fever. You're as cool as a cucumber. But sleep is good before your recital tomorrow."

Except Maddie had no intention of sleeping.

At bedtime, Maddie packed her ballet bag with a flashlight, a baby bottle, goggles, and a kazoo — all the things she'd need to defend Alyssa.

Then Maddie heard something!

It was the CREAK, CREAK sound of someone walking up the stairs!

Maddie tiptoed down the hall and saw Grandma walking into Alyssa's room! Her heart started to beat loudly, ba boom, ba boom.

Grandma was hovering over Alyssa's crib! Maddie quickly pulled out her kazoo and blew loud and hard. Bzzzz! Bzzzz! Bzzzz!
Then she squirted the bottle with all her might.

Grandma screamed. Alyssa cried. Maddie's mother turned on the lights.

"What's going on?" she asked nervously. "Why is Grandma wet? Maddie, what are you doing out of bed? And why do you have your goggles on?"

"I came to save Alyssa!" Maddie shouted proudly. "Grandma was going to eat her!"

Her mother and Grandma both started to laugh.

"What's so funny?" Maddie asked. "Grandma keeps telling Alyssa how delicious she is and how she wants to eat her!"

"Sweetpea," Grandma began, "I would never eat your baby sister or harm her in any way. Calling her delicious is my way of expressing how much I love her. I said the same things to you when you were a baby. Honestly, muffin, I don't bite."

Maddie wasn't convinced. "But what were you doing in Alyssa's room?"

"I was only checking on her," Grandma said softly.

"I'm sorry, Grandma."

Grandma smiled. "Well, you certainly did get yourself into a pickle, but I am proud of you for defending your little sister. Now, sweet dreams my little ballerina."

"I can't wait to see you on stage tomorrow, Maddie. I bet you'll be the shiniest apple of the bunch."